Welles-Turner Memorial Library

2407 Main Street
Glastonbury, Connecticut 06033

In memory of

Joyce Franceschina

The Cocktail Garden

hardie grant books

The Cocktail Garden

BOTANICAL COCKTAILS FOR EVERY SEASON

ILLUSTRATIONS ADRIANA PICKER
RECIPES ED LOVEDAY

Foreword

Listen close, gentle reader. There are places in the world where cocktails are meted out with eye-droppers and lab equipment, where no laughter colours the air and the meticulous rules over the merry.

Perhaps these places are run by people who don't quite grasp that, while certainty is a fine thing in a recipe, the essence of conviviality is about possibility. Those days that become nights. Those nights when one plus one equals something much more interesting than two.

This is where Ed Loveday and Adriana Picker come in. Artists of the palate and palette, respectively, who have a rich appreciation for the finer things in life, for good things done well. And they're never going to tell you not to drink that drink out of a shoe. (They may even have a better shoe for that particular drink.)

While there are people in this world whose dedication to the craft of the cocktail blinds them to the essential art of having a gay old time, rest assured Adriana and Ed are not those people. They don't sell those kinds of vibes and this is not that kind of book.

This book is dedicated to fun.

Inside flourish rare blossoms and blooms of unusual charm. Its fruits are many, and they are here to be shared.

At each turn, Ed distills the essence of fragrant blossoms, fruits and so many other seasonal delights into the glass, mystery and magic intact, while Adriana conjures illustrations that surprise, thrill, inspire, delight and just occasionally mystify.

Whether you're joining this book's keepers by the fire, for a garden party, by the fallen leaves or simply on an endless summer's day, I think you're going to enjoy their company.

PAT NOURSE, *Gourmet Traveller*

Introduction

Cocktails may not be the drinks you turn to on an average weeknight, or even on most weekends. For many they occupy that delicious category of special occasions — parties and celebrations, of course, but also lazy lunches and dinners with friends, afternoons sitting about in the sun, and holidays — fireside or poolside.

But if you chose to give cocktails a little more attention, you might start wondering why they can't feature in an average weeknight at home, or at least on an average weekend . . . The combination of a special spirit from a far-flung corner of the world with seasonal ingredients such as fruits and herbs, and simple mixers like soda water (club soda) or tonic (no soft drink in sight here!), is pure delight.

You won't find any wizardry in this book; there are no beakers, lab coats or dry ice. These are pure and simple flavour-driven cocktails, using produce at the height of its season.

Cocktails are, of course, a step up from a mixed drink. They usually have more than two ingredients, and a simple but elegant garnish or presentation (which at home you might prefer to think of as optional).

While wines of almost any variety can feature in a cocktail, it is spirits — those pure distilled liquors, such as whisky or vodka — that are the key territory of cocktails.

No wonder the world of cocktails is dazzling; this realm of spirits is so dazzling to begin with. Whereas terroir is of high importance in wine, in spirits so many different ingredients come into play, plus craft, plus history. The many unique flavours they carry practically beg for creativity.

These recipes feature fruits, vegetables, flowers and herbs, including some you may not have heard of (and may suddenly feel compelled to plant in your garden!). Pineapple sage, lemon myrtle, honeysuckle, red-veined sorrel . . .

Each recipe serves one — but can be multiplied to make two or even three drinks at a time.

Yes, cocktails can seem frivolous at first, but let yourself be seduced by these drinks spiked with pear and green tea purée, hibiscus syrup and muddled persimmon, and you might start to see that frivolousness is where pleasure resides.

Equipment

IT CAN BE EASY TO GET CARRIED AWAY WITH BAR EQUIPMENT, ESPECIALLY WITH SOME OF THE BEAUTIFULLY MADE PROFESSIONAL GEAR AVAILABLE ONLINE. BUT LET'S KEEP THINGS REAL: YOU REALLY ONLY NEED A FEW KEY ITEMS TO MAKE EVERY RECIPE IN THIS BOOK.

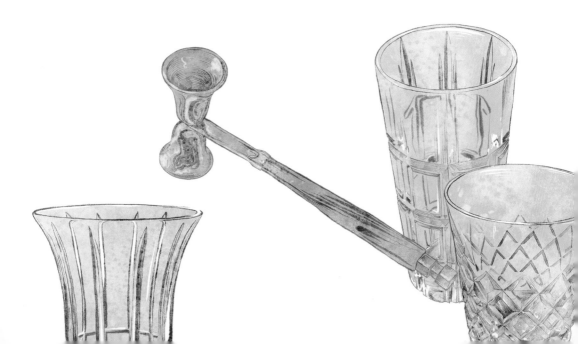

SHAKERS

You're going to need one! (But if you haven't got a shaker yet, or are without access to one, don't be afraid to improvise with what you've got — a jar or even a plastic container will get you going.) Here are three different types of shakers you'll see around:

COBBLER SHAKER The most iconic and readily available cocktail shaker. Three pieces — cup, lid with an in-built strainer, and cap. Downside? It's a bit of a nightmare to use. When the metal pieces get frosty, they contract and get stuck together. Okay for single use, but probably the least convenient style for rapid and high-consumption cocktail making.

BOSTON Perhaps the most versatile system, consisting of a metal cup and a tempered mixing glass. You'll see it in many cocktail bars. An advantage of the boston is that you can watch what you're doing as you add ingredients to the glass. Once you've finished, put the metal cup on top. Use the heel of your hand to give it a whack, pushing it down onto the glass and sealing them together (they usually seal best when the metal cup sits on top of the glass on an angle, forming one nearly straight side). After shaking, unseal the shaker by turning the straight-edged side towards you. Hold the shaker with one hand and gently whack the side of the metal cup with your other hand to break the seal. The only downside to the boston is you're bound to break the glass at some point. It happens to the best of us!

TOBY TINS Very similar to the boston except it's two tins; one smaller and one larger. Sometimes preferred because it is lighter and sturdier than the other shakers (good luck breaking it!). Seal and unseal in exactly the same way as the boston.

STRAINERS

You'll need two types of strainers:

HAWTHORNE STRAINER This strainer is generally made of stainless steel and resembles a small plate with medium-sized holes and a handle. It has a wire coil running around the edge. The coil sits down inside your shaker or mixing glass, holding the strainer firmly in place while you pour. This strainer is mainly used to remove ice and larger solids. (If you don't have a hawthorne strainer, you can make do with a large jar lid placed over your shaker or glass leaving a small gap, to hold back ice and solids.)

TEA/FINE STRAINER Simply hold this over the top of your serving glass as you pour from your shaker or mixing glass. This strainer is often used together with a hawthorne strainer in cocktails served in martini or coupe glasses — the hawthorne strainer holds back the ice and large solids, while the tea strainer filters the small pieces of fruit and other ingredients for a very smooth and refined finish. This is commonly termed 'double straining'.

The Cocktail Garden

MUDDLER

Some drinks will call for fruit to be 'muddled' (pressed, squashed, smashed). Muddlers come in wood, plastic or metal; simple ones resemble a straight-ended rolling pin, or they can have a texture on the base that helps crush ingredients. A small straight-ended rolling pin is a great stand-by if you don't have a dedicated muddler.

MIXING GLASS

For cocktails that call for stirring, not shaking, you'll need a mixing glass. (Some simple cocktails can actually be stirred in their serving glass, but others require a mixing glass for the best presentation.) Mixing glasses look like large glass tumblers with spouts. Any medium-sized glass pitcher or jug will do the trick. Just make sure it's big enough to fit enough ice to chill the drink down.

BAR SPOON

Bar spoons are essentially teaspoons with long handles. There are an infinite number of styles available online, but for bonus functionality look for one with a small flat plate at the end of the handle, which you can also use to lightly muddle herbs or soft fruits.

JIGGER

A jigger is just something to measure out liquids — a conical metal measuring cup. They come in a range of sizes and styles and are designed so that the top and bottom of the cup can be used to measure two different quantities. You don't necessarily need a professional bar jigger; a plastic measuring cup used for measuring medicine is fine, as are kitchen measuring spoons and cups. You simply want to be able to measure in small increments from 10 ml (¼ fl oz) upwards. A teaspoon is handy for measurements under that.

COCKTAIL PICKS

These small, decorative picks are used for threading on garnishes such as blueberries, olives and the like. They are usually made of metal or bamboo and come in all manner of lengths and styles.

Serving Glasses

HIGHBALL GLASS
A tall tumbler.
Any tall glass will do.

ROCKS GLASS
A short tumbler also known a
an 'old-fashioned' glass (name
after the cocktail). Any shor
glass will do in cocktails callin
for a rocks glass.

WINE GLASSES
AND CHAMPAGNE FLUTES
These glasses are used to
serve many cocktails.

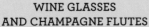

The Cocktail Garden

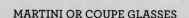

MARTINI OR COUPE GLASSES

These glasses can generally be used interchangeably. While the martini glass has straight sides, the coupe glass looks like a short, wide wine glass on a long stem.

HURRICANE GLASS

A large glass somewhere between a wine glass and a tall glass. Shaped like a vase and on a short stem.

COLLINS GLASS

A very tall and slender tumbler. If you don't have a glass matching this description, any other tall glass will do.

Syrups, Purées, Tinctures & Infusions

SYRUPS ARE NOT JUST SWEETENERS AND FLAVOUR MODIFIERS – THEY'RE ALSO THE PERFECT WAY TO PRESERVE A SEASON'S PRODUCE. THINK OF BEING ABLE TO ENJOY THE FLAVOUR OF STRAWBERRIES OR FIGS AFTER THEIR PRECIOUS SEASONS ARE OVER (IN COCKTAIL OR SODA FORM). MANY OF THESE RECIPES CAN BE FROZEN TO LAST THROUGH THE YEAR.

MAKE SURE YOU TAKE A LOOK AT THE SECTION ON COLD-PROCESS SYRUPS (PAGE 22). IN A BAR THESE MIGHT BE MADE USING A CRYOVAC MACHINE, BUT YOU CAN REPLICATE THIS AT HOME WITH A SIMPLE ZIP-LOCK BAG. THESE SYRUPS ARE MADE WITHOUT HEAT, SO THEY EXTRACT A FRESHER FLAVOUR FROM THE FRUITS, HERBS AND SPICES YOU'RE USING. CONVENTIONAL HOT-PROCESS SYRUPS (PAGE 18) CAN SOMETIMES TASTE A LITTLE STEWED AND JAMMY, WHICH IS NOT ENTIRELY UNDESIRABLE – SOMETIMES THAT'S WHAT YOU'RE AFTER – BUT TRY A COLD-PROCESS SYRUP FOR YOURSELF AND TASTE THE DIFFERENCE. MANY OF THESE RECIPES ALSO WORK REALLY WELL IN NON-ALCOHOLIC DRINKS.

YOU CAN THINK OF TINCTURES (PAGE 28) – LIKE BITTERS – AS THE SEASONINGS OF THE COCKTAIL WORLD. THEY'RE A CONCENTRATED ALCOHOL INFUSION, USUALLY FEATURING JUST ONE PARTICULAR FLAVOUR. THERE'S A UNIVERSE OF TINCTURE POSSIBILITIES, BUT THREE FAVOURITE RECIPES ARE INCLUDED HERE TO GET YOU STARTED.

Hot-Process Syrups

SUGAR SYRUP

240 G (8½ OZ) SUGAR

125 ML (4¼ FL OZ/½ CUP) WATER

Combine the sugar and water in a saucepan and heat gently until all the sugar has dissolved. Allow to cool. This syrup can be stored in a jar or bottle in the refrigerator for up to 1 month.

MAKES 250 ML (8½ FL OZ/1 CUP)

~

A bartender's most important 'mother sauce'. Recipes commonly call for equal parts sugar to water, but using 2 parts sugar to 1 part water (as used here) will dilute your drinks less.

HONEY SYRUP

125 ML (4¼ FL OZ/½ CUP) WATER

350 G (12½ OZ/1 CUP) HONEY

Bring the water to the boil in a saucepan. Add the honey and stir to dissolve. Allow to cool. This syrup can be stored in a jar or bottle in the refrigerator for up to 1 month.

MAKES 375 ML (12¾ FL OZ/1½ CUPS)

~

Honey is such a great flavour to use in cocktails, and works especially well with many brown spirits. However, it's notoriously difficult to mix, often getting stuck to the insides of glasses and shakers. This honey syrup is an easy solution.

The Cocktail Garden

HIBISCUS SYRUP

240 G (8½ OZ) SUGAR

70 G (2½ OZ) DRIED HIBISCUS FLOWERS

ZEST OF ½ LEMON, CUT OFF IN STRIPS

SLICE OF GINGER

1 STAR ANISE

¼ VANILLA BEAN, SPLIT LENGTHWAYS AND SEEDS SCRAPED

500 ML (17 FL OZ/2 CUPS) WATER

Combine all the ingredients in a saucepan and bring to the boil, stirring until the sugar dissolves. Reduce the heat and simmer, uncovered, for 10 minutes. Allow to cool before passing through a fine-meshed sieve. This syrup can be stored in a jar or bottle in the refrigerator for up to 1 month.

MAKES 575 ML (19½ FL OZ/2⅓ CUPS)

GINGER SYRUP

240 G (8½ OZ) SUGAR

200 G (7 OZ) GINGER, FINELY SLICED

500 ML (17 FL OZ/2 CUPS) WATER

Combine all the ingredients in a saucepan and bring to the boil, stirring until the sugar dissolves. Reduce the heat and simmer, uncovered, for 10 minutes. Allow to cool, then strain off the ginger. This syrup can be stored in a jar or bottle in the refrigerator for up to 1 month.

MAKES 575 ML (19½ FL OZ/2⅓ CUPS)

CHAMOMILE SYRUP

240 G (8½ OZ) SUGAR

250 ML (8½ FL OZ/1 CUP) WATER

1 CUP DRIED CHAMOMILE FLOWERS
   (OR PURE LOOSE-LEAF CHAMOMILE TEA)

Combine the sugar and water in a saucepan and place over medium heat, stirring until the sugar dissolves. Once the mixture is boiling, turn off the heat and add the chamomile flowers. Allow to cool, then strain off the flowers. This syrup can be stored in a jar or bottle in the refrigerator for up to 1 month.

MAKES 400 ML (13½ FL OZ/1⅔ CUPS)

HONEYSUCKLE SYRUP

240 G (8½ OZ) SUGAR

250 ML (8½ FL OZ/1 CUP) WATER

1 CUP HONEYSUCKLE FLOWERS, STEMS REMOVED, GENTLY SHAKEN TO
   REMOVE ANY DIRT OR INSECTS

Combine the sugar and water in a saucepan and place over medium heat, stirring until the sugar dissolves. Once the mixture is boiling, turn off the heat and add the honeysuckle flowers. Allow the syrup to cool, then strain off the flowers. The syrup can be stored in a jar or bottle in the refrigerator for up to 1 month.

MAKES 400 ML (13½ FL OZ/1⅔ CUPS)

The Cocktail Garden

RHUBARB SYRUP

240 G (8½ OZ) SUGAR

200 G (7 OZ) RHUBARB, FINELY SLICED

ZEST OF ¼ LEMON, CUT OFF IN STRIPS

500 ML (17 FL OZ/2 CUPS) WATER

Combine all the ingredients in a saucepan and bring to the boil, stirring until the sugar dissolves. Reduce the heat and simmer, uncovered, for 10 minutes. Allow to cool before passing through a fine-meshed sieve. This syrup can be stored in a jar or bottle in the refrigerator for up to 1 month.

MAKES 575 ML (19½ FL OZ/2⅓ CUPS)

SUGAR SNAP-PEA SYRUP

200 ML (6¾ FL OZ) WATER

200 G (7 OZ) SUGAR

100 G (3½ OZ) SUGAR-SNAP PEAS, ROUGHLY CHOPPED

Combine all the ingredients in a saucepan and place over medium heat, stirring until the sugar dissolves. Remove the pan from the heat when the mixture boils. Allow to cool before passing through a fine-meshed sieve. The syrup should be bright green, and can be stored in a jar or bottle in the refrigerator for up to 1 month.

MAKES 350 ML (11¾ FL OZ/1⅓ CUPS)

Cold-Process Syrups

FIG AND THYME SYRUP

500 G (1 LB 2 OZ) FIGS, FINELY SLICED

2 BUNCHES OF THYME

400 G (14 OZ/1¾ CUPS) CASTER (SUPERFINE) SUGAR

Combine all the ingredients in a zip-lock bag, jiggling them around in the bag until well mixed. Press out as much air from the bag as you can, then seal it. Let it sit at room temperature for 24 hours, gently pressing it from time to time and shuffling the ingredients to help dissolve the sugar. Strain the syrup through a fine-meshed sieve, discarding the solids. The syrup can be stored in a jar or bottle in the refrigerator for up to 1 month.

MAKES 450 ML (15¼ FL OZ/1¾ CUPS)

PINEAPPLE AND TANGELO SYRUP

250 G (9 OZ) TANGELO

250 G (9 OZ) PINEAPPLE, PEELED AND ROUGHLY CHOPPED

500 G (1 LB 2 OZ) CASTER (SUPERFINE) SUGAR

Grate the zest of the tangelo, then peel the fruit. Finely chop the flesh. Combine the zest and flesh, pineapple and sugar in a zip-lock bag, jiggling them around in the bag until well mixed. Press out as much air from the bag as you can, then seal it. Let it sit at room temperature for 24 hours, gently pressing from time to time and shuffling the ingredients to help dissolve the sugar. Strain the syrup through a fine-meshed sieve, discarding the solids. The syrup can be stored in a jar or bottle in the refrigerator for up to 1 month.

MAKES 500 ML (17 FL OZ/2 CUPS)

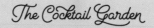

GRAPEFRUIT SYRUP

500 G (1 LB 2 OZ) GRAPEFRUIT

500 G (1 LB 2 OZ) CASTER (SUPERFINE) SUGAR

Grate the zest of the grapefruit, then cut off the remaining skin and pith. Finely chop the flesh. Combine the zest, flesh and sugar in a zip-lock bag, jiggling them around in the bag until well mixed. Press out as much air from the bag as you can, then seal it. Let it sit at room temperature for 24 hours, gently pressing from time to time and shuffling the ingredients to help dissolve the sugar. Strain the syrup through a fine-meshed sieve, discarding the solids. The syrup can be stored in a jar or bottle in the refrigerator for up to 1 month.

MAKES 500 ML (17 FL OZ/2 CUPS)

~

Grapefruit syrup is one of the most versatile syrups you can make. It provides zesty punch in the Curry Leaf Paloma (page 112), and also pairs well with gin and white rum. Or you can enjoy it in a non-alcoholic soda with a hit of fresh citrus.

RASPBERRY SYRUP

500 G (1 LB 2 OZ) RASPBERRIES

400 G (14 OZ/1¾ CUPS) CASTER (SUPERFINE) SUGAR

Combine the raspberries and sugar in a zip-lock bag, jiggling them around in the bag until well mixed. Press out as much air from the bag as you can, then seal it. Let it sit at room temperature for 24 hours, gently pressing from time to time and shuffling the ingredients to help dissolve the sugar. Strain the syrup through a fine-meshed sieve, discarding the solids. The syrup can be stored in a jar or bottle in the refrigerator for up to 1 month.

MAKES 400 ML (13½ FL OZ/1¾ CUPS)

~

There's perhaps no syrup more satisfying to make than your own raspberry syrup. While of course it is great in cocktails, it is also perfect just with soda water (club soda) and a good kick of freshly squeezed lime. And for a slightly more sophisticated non-alcoholic drink, try this raspberry and yuzu soda: combine 30 ml (1 fl oz) raspberry syrup, 15 ml (½ fl oz) lemon juice, 15 ml (½ fl oz) yuzu juice (or more lemon if yuzu is unavailable) and 150 ml (5 fl oz) soda water in a short glass. Stir gently, add ice and garnish with a slice of lemon.

STRAWBERRY AND TARRAGON SYRUP

500 G (1 LB 2 OZ) STRAWBERRIES, HULLED AND FINELY CHOPPED

500 G (1 LB 2 OZ) CASTER (SUPERFINE) SUGAR

⅓ CUP TARRAGON LEAVES

Combine all the ingredients in a zip-lock bag, jiggling them around in the bag until well mixed. Press out as much air from the bag as you can, then seal it. Let it sit at room temperature for 24 hours, gently pressing from time to time and shuffling the ingredients to help dissolve the sugar. Strain the syrup through a fine-meshed sieve, discarding the solids. The syrup can be stored in a jar or bottle in the refrigerator for up to 1 month.

MAKES 500 ML (17 FL OZ/2 CUPS)

The Cocktail Garden

KAFFIR LIME SYRUP

GRATED ZEST OF 10 KAFFIR LIMES
500 G (1 LB 2 OZ) LIMES, PEEL CUT OFF, FLESH FINELY CHOPPED
500 G (1 LB 2 OZ) CASTER (SUPERFINE) SUGAR

Combine the kaffir lime zest and lime flesh with the sugar in a zip-lock bag, jiggling them around in the bag until well mixed. Press out as much air from the bag as you can, then seal it. Let it sit at room temperature for 24 hours, gently pressing from time to time and shuffling the ingredients to help dissolve the sugar. Strain the syrup through a fine-meshed sieve, discarding the solids. The syrup can be stored in a jar or bottle in the refrigerator for up to 1 month.

MAKES 500 ML (17 FL OZ/2 CUPS)

~

This syrup mixes the zest of small, bumpy kaffir limes with the flesh of regular limes. (If kaffir limes are unavailable, you can use regular limes for both elements, although it won't have that unique kaffir lime flavour, which mixes lime, lemon, mandarin and lemongrass. And you usually can't use kaffir limes for their juice as their flesh is dry.) The syrup is a delicious addition to cocktails, and also great for non-drinkers — for the ultimate lime soda, combine 1 part syrup with 4 parts soda water (club soda), plus a squeeze of fresh lime and a sprig of mint.

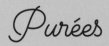

PRESERVED LEMON PURÉE

2 PRESERVED LEMONS, FLESH AND PITH DISCARDED

200 ML (6¾ FL OZ) SUGAR SYRUP (PAGE 18)

Combine the preserved lemon pieces and sugar syrup in a food processor or blender and blitz on high until smooth. The purée can be stored in a jar or bottle in the refrigerator for up to 1 month.

MAKES 310 ML (10½ FL OZ/1¼ CUPS)

SPICED PUMPKIN PURÉE

500 G (1 LB 2 OZ) PUMPKIN (WINTER SQUASH), PEELED
   AND ROUGHLY CHOPPED

½ TEASPOON GROUND CINNAMON

½ TEASPOON GROUND GINGER

¼ TEASPOON FRESHLY GRATED NUTMEG

¼ TEASPOON GROUND ALLSPICE

100 ML (3½ FL OZ) SUGAR SYRUP (PAGE 18)

Toss the pumpkin with the spices on a non-stick baking tray (or a tray lined with baking paper). Spread the pumpkin evenly across the tray. Bake at 180°C (350°F) for 30–45 minutes, or until soft. Leave to cool, then combine the pumpkin and sugar syrup in a food processor or blender and blitz on high until smooth. The purée can be stored in a jar or bottle in the refrigerator for up to 1 week.

MAKES 600 ML (20¼ FL OZ/2⅓ CUPS)

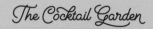

APRICOT, NECTARINE OR PLUM PURÉE

500 G (1 LB 2 OZ) APRICOTS, NECTARINES, OR ANY VARIETY OF
  PLUMS, STONED AND ROUGHLY CHOPPED
100 ML (3½ FL OZ) SUGAR SYRUP (PAGE 18)

Combine the fruit and syrup in a food processor and blitz on high until smooth. The purée can be stored in a jar or bottle in the refrigerator for up to 1 week.

MAKES 580 ML (19½ FL OZ/2⅓ CUPS)

PEAR AND GREEN TEA PURÉE

500 G (1 LB 2 OZ) PEARS, PEELED, CORED AND FINELY DICED
50 G (1¾ OZ) SUGAR
25 ML (¾ FL OZ) WATER
1 TEASPOON MATCHA (JAPANESE GREEN TEA POWDER)

Cook the pears with the sugar and water until soft, then allow to cool. Combine the pears (and their juices) with the matcha in a food processor or blender and blitz on high until smooth. The purée can be stored in a jar or bottle in the refrigerator for up to 1 week.

MAKES 570 ML (19¼ FL OZ/2¼ CUPS)

Tinctures

WALNUT TINCTURE

125 ml (4¼ fl oz/½ cup) 100-PROOF (OR HIGHER) VODKA

70 g (2½ oz) WALNUTS, FINELY CHOPPED

Combine the vodka and walnuts in a sealable jar and leave in a cool, dark place for about 1 week, stirring and tasting each day. The tincture should develop a strong walnut flavour, but be careful it doesn't become bitter. Strain through muslin (cheesecloth) or through a coffee filter paper, discarding the walnuts. Store in a small bottle in the refrigerator, where the tincture will last for months if not years.

MAKES 110 ml (3¾ fl oz/just under ½ cup)

~

When making tinctures, use the highest-proof spirit you can get your hands on, as it will extract more flavour from your ingredient (in this case, walnuts). Use a dropper or an atomiser — or alternatively a teaspoon — to add tinctures to drinks in very small doses.

CARDAMOM TINCTURE

70 g (2½ oz) CARDAMOM PODS

125 ml (4¼ fl oz/½ cup) 100-PROOF (OR HIGHER) VODKA

Lightly toast the cardamom pods in a dry pan over low heat until aromatic. Use a mortar and pestle to split open the pods. Remove the husks, then grind the seeds. Combine the ground cardamom and the vodka in a sealable jar and leave in a cool, dark place for 5–6 days, stirring and tasting each day. The tincture should develop a strong cardamom flavour, but be careful it doesn't become bitter. Strain through muslin (cheesecloth) or through a coffee filter paper. Store in a small bottle in the refrigerator, where the tincture will last for months if not years.

MAKES 120 ml (4 fl oz/½ cup)

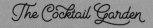

FIG LEAF TINCTURE

125 ML (4¼ FL OZ/½ CUP) 100-PROOF (OR HIGHER) VODKA

5 FIG LEAVES, WASHED, STEMS REMOVED, FINELY CHOPPED

Combine the vodka and fig leaves in a sealable jar and leave in a cool, dark place for 1 week. Strain through muslin (cheesecloth) or through a coffee filter paper. Store in a small bottle in the refrigerator, where the tincture will last for months if not years.

MAKES 115 ML (4 FL OZ/JUST UNDER ½ CUP)

~

The inspiration to make a fig leaf tincture to try in a cocktail came from Analiese Gregory (Ed's business partner and head chef at Bar Brosé in Sydney), when she made a tasty fig leaf custard from leaves gathered from a friend's farm in the Hawkesbury. The flavour of fig leaves is a little hard to describe — it's reminiscent of almond, honey and even coconut — but flavour can be a really personal thing; one person tastes something, while somebody else gets something totally different!

Infusions

BEETROOT GIN

2 MEDIUM BEETROOT (BEETS), PEELED AND FINELY SLICED

300 ML (10¼ FL OZ) GIN

Combine the beetroot slices and gin in a large jar, sealing with a lid. The beetroot colour will bleed into the gin fairly quickly, but for maximum flavour it's best to leave the jar in a cool, dark place for 3 days. Strain out the beetroot and store your infused gin in a bottle in the refrigerator. It should last 1–2 days before losing its vibrant colour due to oxidisation.

MAKES 280 ML (9½ FL OZ / JUST OVER 1 CUP)

~

Use this infused gin to make a beautiful Beetroot Negroni (page 108). It would also make an interesting gin and tonic.

PEACH AND PINEAPPLE-SAGE BOURBON

2 RIPE PEACHES

375 ML (12¾ FL OZ / 1½ CUPS) BOURBON

1 SMALL HANDFUL OF PINEAPPLE SAGE

50 G (1¾ OZ) SUGAR

Stone and roughly chop the peaches. Crack open 1 stone using a mallet or a mortar and pestle, revealing the inner kernel. Place the chopped peach, whole kernel and remaining ingredients in a large jar and seal. Allow to infuse at room temperature for 6 hours, stirring occasionally. Pass the bourbon through a fine-meshed sieve, pressing out as much liquid from the peach solids as possible. Finally, pass through muslin (cheesecloth) or through a coffee filter paper. Store in a bottle in the refrigerator for up to 3 days.

MAKES 375 ML (12¾ FL OZ / 1½ CUPS)

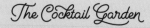

PEAR-INFUSED SCOTCH

2 PEARS, PEELED, CORED AND DICED

½ NUTMEG, ROUGHLY CRUSHED

2 STAR ANISE

½ CINNAMON STICK

¼ VANILLA BEAN, SPLIT LENGTHWAYS AND SEEDS SCRAPED

GRATED ZEST OF ½ ORANGE

375 ML (12¾ FL OZ/1½ CUPS) BLENDED SCOTCH WHISKY

Cook the pears in a very small splash of water until soft, then leave to cool. Lightly toast the nutmeg pieces, star anise and cinnamon stick in a dry pan over low heat until aromatic. Transfer the toasted spices to a large jar and add the pear and remaining ingredients, combining well. Seal and leave in a cool, dark place for 1 week. Pass the scotch through a fine-meshed sieve, pressing out as much liquid from the pear solids as possible. Finally, pass through muslin (cheesecloth) or through a coffee filter paper. Store in a bottle in the refrigerator for 3-4 days.

MAKES 365 ML (12¼ FL OZ/1½ CUPS)

~

You can use pears of any variety in this recipe — even nashi pears.

TEA-INFUSED VODKA

250 ML (8½ FL OZ/1 CUP) VODKA

1 TABLESPOON YUNNAN RED TEA (*DIAN HONG*)

Combine the vodka and tea in a jar and stir. Seal and leave to sit at room temperature for 6 hours. Pass through a fine-meshed sieve. Store in a bottle in the refrigerator, where it will last for months.

MAKES 235 ML (8 FL OZ/JUST UNDER 1 CUP)

BUTTER-WASHED VODKA

125 G (4½ OZ) UNSALTED BUTTER

375 ML (12¾ FL OZ/1½ CUPS) VODKA

Gently heat the butter until just melted. Combine the butter and vodka in a container and stir to combine. Seal and leave to sit at room temperature for 3 hours, then transfer to the refrigerator and leave for 1–2 hours, until the butter has solidified. Scoop off the layer of butter and pass the vodka through a fine-meshed sieve. Store in a bottle in the refrigerator for up to 1 week.

MAKES 375 ML (12¾ FL OZ/1½ CUPS)

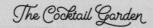

BANANA RUM

1 OVERRIPE BANANA, FINELY CHOPPED

250 ML (8½ FL OZ/1 CUP) AÑEJO RUM

Combine the banana and rum in a jar, sealing with a lid, and leave in a cool, dark place for 1 week. Pass the rum through a fine-meshed sieve, pressing out as much liquid from the banana solids as possible. Finally, pass through muslin (cheesecloth) or through a coffee filter paper. Store in a bottle in the refrigerator for up to 3–4 days.

MAKES 230 ML (7¾ FL OZ/JUST UNDER 1 CUP)

GRAPEFRUIT-INFUSED CAMPARI

375 ML (12¾ FL OZ/1½ CUPS) CAMPARI

GRATED ZEST OF ½ GRAPEFRUIT

Combine the Campari and zest in a jar. Seal and leave to sit at room temperature overnight. Pass through a fine-meshed sieve and store in a bottle in the refrigerator for up to 1 week.

MAKES 375 ML (12¾ FL OZ/1½ CUPS)

For Endless Days

T-SHIRT WEATHER, DAYS AT THE BEACH, AND POSSIBILITIES FOR PARTIES, PICNICS AND BARBECUES – SUMMER IS THE STUFF DREAMS ARE MADE OF, ESPECIALLY AT OTHER TIMES OF THE YEAR. ADD TO THIS ALL THE BEAUTIFUL SUMMER PRODUCE, AND THOSE ICY COCKTAILS WITH RUM/TEQUILA/GIN THAT REALLY HIT THE SPOT.

MANGOES, PEACHES AND BERRIES (AND MUCH MORE) ARE RIPE FOR THE PICKING. IN THE COCKTAIL KITCHEN THEY SPELL OUT ALL MANNER OF COLD DRINKS, PERFECT FOR COOLING YOU DOWN ON THOSE HOT DAYS AND HOTTER NIGHTS.

WHEN RASPBERRIES ARE AT THEIR PEAK, YOU SHOULD JUMP ON THEM, AND BAG THEM UP WITH SOME SUGAR IN THE SIMPLE COLD-PROCESS SYRUP ON PAGE 24. THIS SYRUP IS SO VIBRANT COMPARED WITH A COOKED SYRUP, AND THE ULTIMATE GIFT TO YOURSELF (AND IT'S NOT ALWAYS ABOUT ALCOHOL, AS THIS SYRUP IS GREAT IN NON-ALCOHOLIC SODAS).

DID YOU KNOW THAT MARGARITAS ARE A GREAT MATCH FOR MARGHERITAS (PAGE 48)? OR THAT MANGO GOES WITH MATCHA (PAGE 60)? OR THAT A COBBLER IS NOT ONLY A DELICIOUS SUMMER PUDDING, BUT ALSO A COCKTAIL (PAGE 56)? (IN FACT, IT'S A RATHER OLD COCKTAIL, BUT THERE'S A TASTY VERSION WITH BERRIES IN THIS CHAPTER.)

Endless Summer

½ WHITE PEACH, PLUS A WEDGE TO GARNISH

45 ML (1½ FL OZ) VODKA

15 ML (½ FL OZ) APEROL

15 ML (½ FL OZ) YUZU JUICE (SEE NOTE BELOW)

15 ML (½ FL OZ) LEMON JUICE

15 ML (½ FL OZ) SUGAR SYRUP (PAGE 18)

SPRIG OF MINT TO GARNISH

Muddle the peach in the bottom of a shaker. Add the remaining ingredients except the garnishes and shake with ice. Pass through a small fine-meshed strainer into a rocks or short glass containing fresh ice. Garnish with the wedge of peach and sprig of mint.

~

If you're lucky enough to have access to fresh yuzu (a small Japanese citrus), give yourself a high five and stop reading! If you don't, bottled yuzu juice can be found at Japanese grocers. Otherwise, replace with grapefruit juice, or forgo entirely and double the lemon juice.

FOR ENDLESS DAYS

The Cocktail Garden

Raspberry Beret

45 ML (1½ FL OZ) WHITE RUM

10 ML (¼ FL OZ) CAMPARI

30 ML (1 FL OZ) LIME JUICE

30 ML (1 FL OZ) PINEAPPLE JUICE

20 ML (¾ FL OZ) SUGAR SYRUP (PAGE 18)

4 RASPBERRIES, PLUS 1 TO GARNISH

Shake all the ingredients without ice to create a foam. Add ice and shake again. Pass through a small fine-meshed strainer into a martini or coupe glass and garnish with the raspberry on a cocktail pick.

Blueberry Smash

5-6 BLUEBERRIES, PLUS EXTRA TO GARNISH

60 ML (2 FL OZ) GIN

30 ML (1 FL OZ) LIME JUICE

6 THAI BASIL LEAVES

20 ML (¾ FL OZ) SUGAR SYRUP (PAGE 18)

Muddle the blueberries in the bottom of a shaker. Add the remaining ingredients and shake hard with ice. Pass through a small fine-meshed strainer into a martini or coupe glass and garnish with a cocktail pick of blueberries.

The Cocktail Garden

FOR ENDLESS DAYS

41

Watermelon Margarita

½ TEASPOON *SHICHIMI TOGARASHI* (JAPANESE SEVEN SPICE,
  SEE NOTE BELOW)

½ TEASPOON SEA SALT

WEDGE OF LIME, PLUS 30 ML (1 FL OZ) LIME JUICE

60 ML (2 FL OZ) BLANCO TEQUILA

45 ML (1½ FL OZ) WATERMELON JUICE

10 ML (¼ FL OZ) SUGAR SYRUP (PAGE 18)

Combine the *shichimi togarashi* and salt in a shallow bowl and mix well. Wipe the lime wedge around the outside rim of a martini or coupe glass to wet it. Tilt the bowl slightly so the spice mixture gathers up one end, and dip and turn the rim of the glass in the spice until it is coated all around. Shake off any excess. Shake all the remaining ingredients with ice, then pass through a small fine-meshed strainer into the glass.

~

Shichimi togarashi is a Japanese spice mix featuring chilli and other interesting spices typically sold in small, red-capped shakers. You should be able to find it in most Asian grocers.

Cherry Pisco Sour

4 CHERRIES, HALVED AND PITTED, PLUS AN EXTRA CHERRY TO GARNISH

60 ML (2 FL OZ) PISCO

30 ML (1 FL OZ) LEMON JUICE

20 ML (¾ FL OZ) SUGAR SYRUP (PAGE 18)

1-2 TEASPOONS EGG WHITE

2 DASHES OF BITTERS (PREFERABLY PEYCHAUD'S)

Muddle the cherries in the bottom of a shaker. Add the remaining ingredients and shake without ice to create a foam. Shake again with ice. Pass through a small fine-meshed strainer into a martini or coupe glass. Garnish with a whole cherry.

FOR ENDLESS DAYS

Tiki Monk

2 SMALL CHUNKS OF PINEAPPLE

30 ML (1 FL OZ) AÑEJO RUM

30 ML (1 FL OZ) YELLOW CHARTREUSE

30 ML (1 FL OZ) LIME JUICE, PLUS A WHEEL TO GARNISH

15 ML (½ FL OZ) PINEAPPLE GUM SYRUP, OR PINEAPPLE
AND TANGELO SYRUP (PAGE 22)

3 DASHES OF BITTERS (PREFERABLY ANGOSTURA)

Muddle the pineapple in the bottom of a shaker. Add the remaining ingredients and shake with ice. Pass through a small fine-meshed strainer into a martini or coupe glass and float the lime wheel on top.

~

'Tiki' is a tropical category of cocktails generally made with rum, fruit such as pineapple, and sometimes spices. This one contains Chartreuse, a liqueur invented by French monks. Thus, the Tiki Monk! It also uses homemade fruit syrup, or alternatively pineapple gum syrup, which you can buy in small bottles. (Gum syrup is sugar syrup containing a resin known as gum arabic, which adds viscosity and silkiness to cocktails; pineapple gum syrup is simply gum syrup infused with pineapple.)

Margherita Margarita

SEA SALT

WEDGE OF LIME, PLUS 30 ML (1 FL OZ) LIME JUICE

60 ML (2 FL OZ) REPOSADO TEQUILA

30 ML (1 FL OZ) TOMATO JUICE

3–4 BASIL LEAVES

15 ML (½ FL OZ) SUGAR SYRUP (PAGE 18)

1 CHERRY TOMATO TO GARNISH

Put a little salt in a shallow bowl. Wipe the lime wedge around the outside rim of a martini or coupe glass to wet it. Tilt the bowl slightly so the salt gathers up one end, and dip and turn the rim of the glass in the salt until it is coated all around. Shake off any excess. Combine the remaining ingredients except the cherry tomato in a shaker with ice, and shake. Pass through a small fine-meshed strainer into the glass. Garnish with the cherry tomato on a cocktail pick.

~

Put this margarita containing tomato and basil on the menu at your next pizza night (especially if you're making margheritas!).

The Cocktail Garden

FOR ENDLESS DAYS

Apricot Sour

40 ML (1¼ FL OZ) AÑEJO RUM

20 ML (¾ FL OZ) AMONTILLADO SHERRY

30 ML (1 FL OZ) LEMON JUICE

30 ML (1 FL OZ) APRICOT PURÉE (PAGE 27)

WHEEL OF FRESH APRICOT TO GARNISH

Shake all the ingredients, except the wheel of apricot, with ice. Pass through a small fine-meshed strainer into a martini or coupe glass. Float the wheel of apricot on top.

FOR ENDLESS DAYS

Warm Summer Evenings

60 ML (2 FL OZ) FINO SHERRY

45 ML (1½ FL OZ) NECTARINE PURÉE (PAGE 27)

10 ML (¼ FL OZ) SUGAR SYRUP (PAGE 18)

SODA WATER (CLUB SODA)

SPRIG OF BASIL TO GARNISH

Combine the sherry, nectarine purée and sugar syrup in a wine glass. Add ice and top with a dash of soda water, then stir gently. Garnish with the basil.

FOR ENDLESS DAYS

Racquet Club

4 SLICES OF CUCUMBER
HANDFUL OF DICED WATERMELON
45 ML (1½ FL OZ) GIN
15 ML (½ FL OZ) ELDERFLOWER CORDIAL
30 ML (1 FL OZ) LIME JUICE
SPARKLING WHITE WINE
SPRIG OF MINT TO GARNISH

Muddle the cucumber and watermelon in the bottom of a shaker. Add the gin, cordial and lime juice and shake with ice. Pass through a small fine-meshed strainer into a collins or tall glass containing fresh ice and top with sparkling wine. Stir gently, and garnish with the mint.

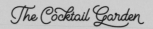

Summer Cobbler

1 RASPBERRY, PLUS EXTRA TO GARNISH

1 BLACKBERRY, PLUS EXTRA TO GARNISH

2 SLICES OF ORANGE, SKIN ON

90 ML (3 FL OZ) AMONTILLADO SHERRY

20 ML (¾ FL OZ) SUGAR SYRUP (PAGE 18)

A FEW REDCURRANTS (OPTIONAL)

SPRIG OF MINT TO GARNISH

¼ TEASPOON ICING (CONFECTIONERS') SUGAR (OPTIONAL)

Muddle the raspberry, blackberry and orange slices in the bottom of a shaker. Add the sherry and sugar syrup and shake with ice. Pass through a small fine-meshed strainer into a collins or tall glass containing fresh crushed ice. Garnish with extra berries, redcurrants (if using) and the mint. For bonus points, dust icing (confectioners') sugar over the top.

~

Sherry cobblers are fantastic drinks throughout the whole year — just use other seasonal fruits when berries are out of season.

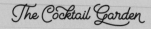

FOR ENDLESS DAYS

Acapulco Bay

45 ML (1½ FL OZ) REPOSADO TEQUILA

15 ML (½ FL OZ) MEZCAL

30 ML (1 FL OZ) LIME JUICE

30 ML (1 FL OZ) SUGAR SYRUP (PAGE 18)

3 CHUNKS OF PINEAPPLE

6 CORIANDER (CILANTRO) LEAVES, PLUS AN EXTRA SPRIG TO GARNISH

1 CUP ICE

HOLLOWED PINEAPPLE TO SERVE (OPTIONAL)

Combine all the ingredients in a blender and blitz until smooth. Pour into a hollowed pineapple (or a collins or tall glass). Garnish with the sprig of coriander.

~

Acapulco Bay is a beachside resort south of Mexico City, and this drink is all things beach and summer and Mexico. Tequila forms the backbone and mezcal provides some underground smokiness.

Mango and Matcha Margarita

½ TEASPOON MATCHA (JAPANESE GREEN TEA POWDER)

1 TEASPOON SEA SALT

WEDGE OF LIME, PLUS 30 ML (1 FL OZ) LIME JUICE

½ MANGO, ROUGHLY CHOPPED

60 ML (2 FL OZ) BLANCO TEQUILA

15 ML (½ FL OZ) SUGAR SYRUP (PAGE 18)

Combine the matcha and salt in a shallow bowl and mix well. Wipe the lime wedge around the outside rim of a martini or coupe glass to wet it. Tilt the bowl slightly so the salt gathers up one end, and dip and turn the rim of the glass in the salt until it is coated all around. Shake off any excess. Muddle the mango in the bottom of a shaker, then add the lime juice, tequila and sugar syrup. Shake with ice, then pass through a small fine-meshed strainer into the glass.

FOR ENDLESS DAYS

Summer G & T

1 FINGER LIME (SEE NOTE BELOW)
30 ML (1 FL OZ) GIN
100 ML (3½ FL OZ) TONIC WATER
SPRIG OF SHISO TO GARNISH (SEE NOTE BELOW)

Cut the finger lime in half. From the ends, gently squeeze the lime 'caviar' into a large wine glass as if squeezing a tube of toothpaste. Add the gin, tonic and some ice and stir gently. Garnish with the shiso.

~

Finger limes are native to Australia. They are cylindrical and roughly finger-like in length, and inside are tiny caviar-like citrus balls. Shiso — also known as perilla — is a Japanese herb that is part of the mint family. The serrated leaves come in green and red (most would consider it purple). It's super aromatic and great in cocktails whenever you want to amp up the freshness.

Peach and Pineapple-Sage Old Fashioned

60 ml (2 fl oz) PEACH AND PINEAPPLE-SAGE BOURBON (PAGE 30)
3 DASHES OF BITTERS (PREFERABLY ANGOSTURA)
STRIP OF LEMON ZEST
SPRIG OF PINEAPPLE SAGE TO GARNISH (SEE NOTE BELOW)

Combine the bourbon and bitters in a mixing glass with ice and stir to chill the mixture. Strain (removing the ice) into a rocks or short glass containing fresh ice. Squeeze the strip of lemon zest to release its oils and add to the glass along with the pineapple sage.

~

Look out for pineapple sage on your next trip to the nursery — this sage variety from Central America has red flowers in autumn (fall) that are a bird magnet. The pointed green leaves are scented somewhat like ripe pineapples and are excellent in tea and cocktails!

The Cocktail Garden

FOR ENDLESS DAYS

Inflatable Flamingo

8 STRAWBERRIES, SLICED, PLUS EXTRA TO SERVE
540 ML (18¼ FL OZ) DRY ROSÉ
125 G (4½ OZ / 1 CUP) RASPBERRIES
270 ML (9¼ FL OZ) GIN
90 ML (3 FL OZ) LEMON JUICE
60 ML (2 FL OZ) SUGAR SYRUP (PAGE 18)
A FEW SPRIGS OF MINT TO GARNISH

Combine the strawberries and rosé in a jar or container and place in the refrigerator to steep overnight. Muddle the raspberries in the bottom of a large pitcher. Strain the rosé over the top, discarding the strawberries. Add the gin, lemon juice and sugar syrup and stir gently. Add ice and some fresh sliced strawberries and mint.

SERVES 6

~

This is the perfect pool party punch. Unlike the other recipes in this book, it's one to make in a big batch. This means less time in the kitchen and more time floating in the pool!

The Cocktail Garden

FOR ENDLESS DAYS

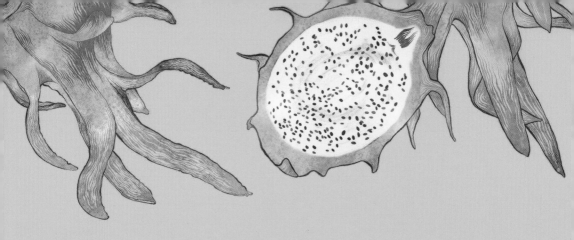

For Adriana

3 LYCHEES

3 SLICES OF DRAGON FRUIT, SKIN ON

60 ML (2 FL OZ) DRY VERMOUTH

15 ML (½ FL OZ) GIN

15 ML (½ FL OZ) LIME JUICE

15 ML (½ FL OZ) LEMON JUICE

PULP OF ½ PASSIONFRUIT

20 ML (¾ FL OZ) SUGAR SYRUP (PAGE 18)

SPRIG OF MINT TO GARNISH

Muddle the lychees and 2 slices of the dragon fruit in the bottom of a shaker. Add the remaining ingredients, except the last slice of dragon fruit and the mint, and shake with ice. Pass through a small fine-meshed strainer into a highball or tall glass containing fresh crushed ice. Add the remaining slice of dragon fruit and the mint.

The Cocktail Garden

FOR ENDLESS DAYS

By the Fallen Leaves

COOKS COMMONLY LIST AUTUMN (FALL) AS THEIR FAVOURITE SEASON – A TIME OF ABUNDANT OVERLAP BETWEEN ALL OF SUMMER'S SWEET AND SUN-DRENCHED PRODUCE, WITH HUMBLE PUMPKIN (WINTER SQUASH), PEARS AND APPLES COMING INTO SEASON TO SEE US RIGHT THROUGH THE COOLER MONTHS. IT'S A BRILLIANT TIME FOR MAKING COCKTAILS, TOO.

FIGS ARE THE SEED-STUDDED JEWELS OF THE SEASON, AND MIGHT HAVE YOU THINKING OF PIZZAS, SALADS AND DESSERTS – OR COILING THEM UP INSIDE A SLIVER OF PROSCIUTTO – BUT MAKING A COLD-PROCESS SYRUP OF FIGS (PAGE 22) IS THE ULTIMATE CELEBRATION OF THE FRUIT IN DRINK FORM. EVEN THE LEAVES CAN BE USED AS A FLAVOURING, ADDING A SIMPLE YET UNEXPECTED TWIST TO A MARTINI (PAGE 92).

SOME OF THE OTHER AUTUMN INGREDIENTS THAT BEG TO BE MUDDLED OR BLENDED INTO A COCKTAIL INCLUDE PLUMS, GRAPES, KIWI FRUIT, PERSIMMONS AND EVEN PUMPKIN.

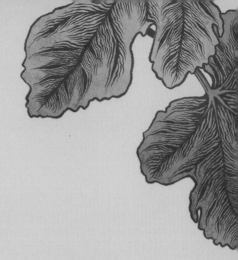

Fig and Thyme Cooler

60 ML (2 FL OZ) DRY VERMOUTH

30 ML (1 FL OZ) LEMON JUICE

30 ML (1 FL OZ) FIG AND THYME SYRUP (PAGE 22)

45 ML (1½ FL OZ) SODA WATER (CLUB SODA)

SPRIG OF THYME TO GARNISH

Shake the vermouth, lemon juice and fig syrup with ice. Strain (removing the ice) into a highball or tall glass containing fresh ice. Top with the soda water and stir gently. Garnish with the thyme.

~

The only problem with figs is that their season is short! Make a big batch of Fig and thyme syrup and freeze it so you can enjoy the flavour of figs well after they've come and gone. Thyme is a classic pairing with the fruit, but you can play around with other herbs too.

BY THE FALLEN LEAVES

Ume Sour

½ BLOOD PLUM, PLUS A FINELY SLICED WHEEL TO GARNISH

45 ML (1½ FL OZ) BLENDED SCOTCH WHISKY

15 ML (½ FL OZ) *UMESHU* (JAPANESE PLUM WINE)

30 ML (1 FL OZ) LEMON JUICE

15 ML (½ FL OZ) SUGAR SYRUP (PAGE 18)

1–2 TEASPOONS EGG WHITE

Muddle the plum in the bottom of a shaker, then add the remaining ingredients. Shake without ice first, to create a foam. Then shake again with ice. Pass through a small fine-meshed strainer into a wine glass and serve neat with the wheel of plum floating on top.

The Cocktail Garden

BY THE FALLEN LEAVES

75

Two Bridges

40 ML (1¼ FL OZ) RYE WHISKY

15 ML (½ FL OZ) AVERNA

10 ML (¼ FL OZ) ROSSO VERMOUTH

1 TEASPOON WALNUT TINCTURE (PAGE 28)

1 MARASCHINO CHERRY TO GARNISH

Combine all the ingredients, except the cherry, in a mixing glass. Add ice and stir to chill the mixture. Strain (removing the ice) into a martini or coupe glass and garnish with the cherry.

~

This drink garnished with a maraschino cherry is loosely inspired by two favourite classic cocktails — the Manhattan and the Brooklyn. (Two Bridges is a neighbourhood in Manhattan around the footings of the Manhattan and Brooklyn bridges.) When buying maraschino cherries, don't get the toxic fluoro pink stuff — look for a quality brand such as Luxardo.

BY THE FALLEN LEAVES

Pear and Green Tea Bellini

45 ML (1½ FL OZ) PEAR AND GREEN TEA PURÉE (PAGE 27)
90 ML (3 FL OZ) PROSECCO

Gently stir the purée together with most of the Prosecco in a mixing glass. Pour into a flute or wine glass and top with the remaining Prosecco.

The Cocktail Garden

BY THE FALLEN LEAVES

Kiwi Collins

½ KIWI FRUIT, SKIN REMOVED, PLUS AN EXTRA SLICE TO GARNISH

45 ML (1½ FL OZ) VODKA

15 ML (½ FL OZ) AKVAVIT

30 ML (1 FL OZ) LIME JUICE

20 ML (¾ FL OZ) SUGAR SYRUP (PAGE 18)

SPRIG OF DILL TO GARNISH

Muddle the kiwi fruit in the bottom of a shaker. Add the remaining ingredients except dill and shake with ice. Pass through a small fine-meshed strainer into a collins or tall glass containing fresh crushed ice. Add the dill and slice of kiwi fruit.

Sloe Moon Rising

6 RED GRAPES

45 ML (1½ FL OZ) SLOE GIN

15 ML (½ FL OZ) BRÀULIO

30 ML (1 FL OZ) LIME JUICE

1–2 TEASPOONS EGG WHITE

Muddle 5 of the grapes in the bottom of a shaker, saving 1 to garnish. Add the remaining ingredients and shake without ice to create a foam. Shake again with ice. Pass through a small fine-meshed strainer into a martini or coupe glass and garnish with the last grape on a cocktail pick.

The COCKTAIL Garden

BY THE FALLEN LEAVES

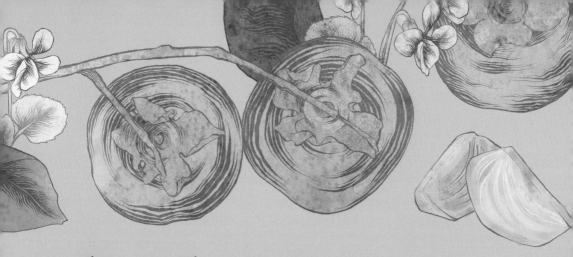

Persimmon Pisco Sour

½ PERSIMMON, PEELED AND ROUGHLY CHOPPED

60 ML (2 FL OZ) PISCO

30 ML (1 FL OZ) LEMON JUICE

20 ML (¾ FL OZ) SUGAR SYRUP (PAGE 18)

1-2 TEASPOONS EGG WHITE

A FEW NATIVE AUSTRALIAN VIOLETS OR OTHER SMALL EDIBLE
FLOWERS TO GARNISH

Muddle the persimmon in the bottom of a shaker. Add the remaining ingredients, except the flowers, and shake without ice to create a foam. Add ice and shake again. Pass through a small fine-meshed strainer into a martini or coupe glass and garnish with the flowers.

The Cocktail Garden

BY THE FALLEN LEAVES

The Cocktail Garden

Apple Smash

45 ML (1½ FL OZ) LAIRD'S APPLEJACK

30 ML (1 FL OZ) APPLE JUICE, PLUS A THIN WEDGE OF APPLE TO GARNISH

15 ML (½ FL OZ) LIME JUICE

15 ML (½ FL OZ) LEMON JUICE

15 ML (½ FL OZ) SUGAR SYRUP (PAGE 18)

SODA WATER (CLUB SODA)

HANDFUL OF THAI BASIL LEAVES, PLUS A LARGE SPRIG TO GARNISH

Shake all the ingredients, except the soda water and garnishes, hard with ice. Strain (removing the ice) into a tall glass containing fresh ice and top with a splash of soda water. Stir gently. Add the apple and sprig of Thai basil.

Spiced Pumpkin Sour

60 ML (2 FL OZ) BOURBON

30 ML (1 FL OZ) LEMON JUICE

40 ML (1¼ FL OZ) SPICED PUMPKIN PURÉE (PAGE 26)

1–2 TEASPOONS EGG WHITE

NUTMEG TO FRESHLY GRATE ON TOP

Combine all the ingredients, except the nutmeg, in a shaker. Shake without ice to create a foam, then add ice and shake again. Pass through a small fine-meshed strainer into a rocks or short glass containing fresh ice and grate a little nutmeg over the top.

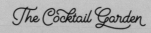

BY THE FALLEN LEAVES

The Cocktail Garden

Pear and Ginger Highball

45 ML (1½ FL OZ) PEAR-INFUSED SCOTCH (PAGE 31)

15 ML (½ FL OZ) AMONTILLADO SHERRY

30 ML (1 FL OZ) LEMON JUICE

30 ML (1 FL OZ) GINGER SYRUP (PAGE 19)

SODA WATER (CLUB SODA)

PIECE OF GLACÉ GINGER TO GARNISH

Shake all the ingredients, except the soda water and glacé ginger, with ice. Strain (removing the ice) into a highball or tall glass containing fresh ice. Top with a dash of soda water and stir gently. Garnish with the glacé ginger.

Fig Leaf Martini

60 ML (2 FL OZ) CHILLED GIN

10 ML (¼ FL OZ) DRY VERMOUTH

3 DROPS (OR ½ TEASPOON) FIG LEAF TINCTURE (PAGE 29)

Combine the gin and vermouth in a mixing glass. Add some large ice cubes and stir to chill the mixture thoroughly. Strain (removing the ice) into a martini or coupe glass and add the fig leaf tincture.

~

No matter how you like your martini — gin, vodka, dry, wet, dirty, stirred or shaken (but does anyone other than James Bond actually drink their martinis shaken?) — there's one universal rule: COLD IS KEY. Keep your spirit of choice in the freezer, or at least in the refrigerator, and use the largest ice cubes you can. This will help chill your martini without diluting it too much.

The Cocktail Garden

BY THE FALLEN LEAVES

Autumn G & T

30 ML (1 FL OZ) GIN
100 ML (3½ FL OZ) TONIC WATER
3 SLICES OF PEAR TO GARNISH
2 STAR ANISE TO GARNISH

Combine the gin and tonic in a large wine glass. Add ice and stir gently, then add the pear slices and star anise.

Plum and Lemon Thyme Apéro

60 ML (2 FL OZ) FINO SHERRY

30 ML (1 FL OZ) PLUM PURÉE (PAGE 27)

30 ML (1 FL OZ) SODA WATER (CLUB SODA)

2 SPRIGS OF LEMON THYME TO GARNISH

Combine the sherry and plum purée in a wine glass. Add ice and stir, then add the soda water and gently stir again. Garnish with the lemon thyme.

~

Apéro, apéritif, aperitivo: *these drinks are one and the same. They're generally consumed in the afternoon or early evening before dinner, and are based on wine, vermouth or amaro (Italian bitter liqueur). They are low in alcohol and super refreshing.*

Tea Mule

60 ML (2 FL OZ) TEA-INFUSED VODKA (PAGE 32)

JUICE OF ½ LIME

GINGER BEER

SLICE OF GINGER TO GARNISH

SPRIG OF MINT TO GARNISH

Pour the vodka into a tall glass over ice. Add the lime juice and fill with ginger beer. Stir, then garnish with the ginger and mint.

By the
Bonfire

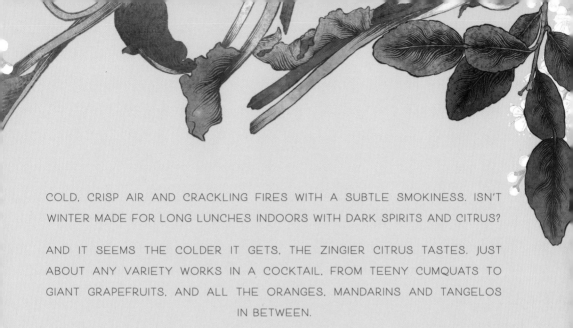

COLD, CRISP AIR AND CRACKLING FIRES WITH A SUBTLE SMOKINESS. ISN'T WINTER MADE FOR LONG LUNCHES INDOORS WITH DARK SPIRITS AND CITRUS?

AND IT SEEMS THE COLDER IT GETS, THE ZINGIER CITRUS TASTES. JUST ABOUT ANY VARIETY WORKS IN A COCKTAIL, FROM TEENY CUMQUATS TO GIANT GRAPEFRUITS, AND ALL THE ORANGES, MANDARINS AND TANGELOS IN BETWEEN.

THERE IS PERHAPS NO BETTER USE OF GRAPEFRUIT THAN IN DRINKS – WHETHER SQUEEZING IT IN FRESH, MAKING THE ZESTY COLD-PROCESS SYRUP ON PAGE 23, OR USING IT TO INFUSE CAMPARI (PAGE 33).

STALWART VEGETABLES SUCH AS CARROT, CELERY AND BEETROOT ARE NOT UNWELCOME IN COCKTAILS, ADDING COLOUR AND EARTHINESS. AND THEN THERE ARE THOSE INGREDIENTS THAT DON'T NEED TO BE ASSOCIATED WITH ANY SEASON AT ALL, BUT SEEM PARTICULARLY FITTING IN THE SPAREST TIME OF YEAR. COFFEE IS PAIRED WITH HONEY, CARDAMOM AND BUTTER-WASHED VODKA IN A COCKTAIL ON PAGE 128, FOR A WARMING TAKE ON THE CLASSIC ESPRESSO MARTINI.

Blood Orange Spritz

20 ML (¾ FL OZ) BRÀULIO

100 ML (3½ FL OZ) PROSECCO

45 ML (1½ FL OZ) BLOOD ORANGE JUICE, PLUS A WHEEL OF BLOOD ORANGE TO GARNISH

10 ML (¼ FL OZ) SUGAR SYRUP (PAGE 18)

1 SAGE LEAF TO GARNISH

Combine the Bràulio, Prosecco, orange juice and sugar syrup in a wine glass. Add ice and stir, then add the orange wheel and sage.

BY THE BONFIRE

Carrot Fix

40 ML (1¼ FL OZ) BOURBON

10 ML (¼ FL OZ) CAMPARI

30 ML (1 FL OZ) LEMON JUICE

45 ML (1½ FL OZ) CARROT JUICE

15 ML (½ FL OZ) SUGAR SYRUP (PAGE 18)

SMALL SPRIG OF DILL TO GARNISH

Shake all the ingredients, except the dill, hard with ice. Pass through a small fine-meshed strainer into a martini or coupe glass and garnish with the dill.

BY THE BONFIRE

Preserved Lemon Margarita

60 ML (2 FL OZ) BLANCO TEQUILA

30 ML (1 FL OZ) LEMON JUICE

30 ML (1 FL OZ) PRESERVED LEMON PURÉE (PAGE 26)

3 DROPS (OR ½ TEASPOON) CARDAMOM TINCTURE (PAGE 28)

DEHYDRATED LEMON WHEEL TO GARNISH

Shake all the ingredients, except the lemon wheel, hard with ice. Pass through a small fine-meshed strainer into a martini or coupe glass and garnish with the lemon wheel.

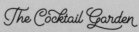

The Cocktail Garden

BY THE BONFIRE

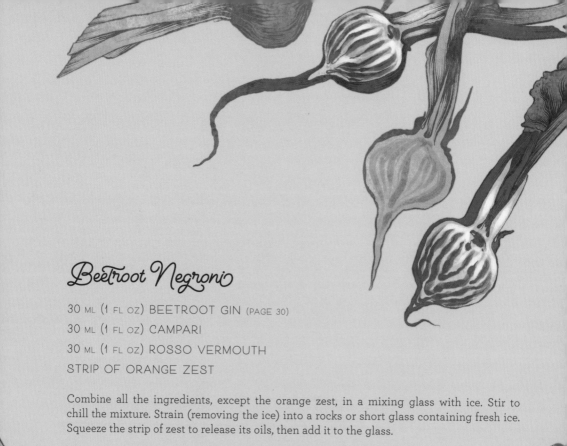

Beetroot Negroni

30 ML (1 FL OZ) BEETROOT GIN (PAGE 30)

30 ML (1 FL OZ) CAMPARI

30 ML (1 FL OZ) ROSSO VERMOUTH

STRIP OF ORANGE ZEST

Combine all the ingredients, except the orange zest, in a mixing glass with ice. Stir to chill the mixture. Strain (removing the ice) into a rocks or short glass containing fresh ice. Squeeze the strip of zest to release its oils, then add it to the glass.

The Cocktail Garden

BY THE BONFIRE

Celery Fizz

60 ML (2 FL OZ) RYE WHISKY

5 ML (¼ FL OZ/1 TEASPOON) ABSINTHE

45 ML (1½ FL OZ) CELERY JUICE

15 ML (½ FL OZ) LEMON JUICE

15 ML (½ FL OZ) LIME JUICE

PINCH OF SALT

SODA WATER (CLUB SODA)

CELERY SEEDS TO GARNISH

Shake all the ingredients, except the soda water and celery seeds, hard with ice. Strain (removing the ice) into a highball or tall glass containing fresh ice. Top with soda water and stir gently. Sprinkle with celery seeds.

~

You can omit the absinthe in this cocktail if you prefer, but it really brings out the 'green' notes in the celery.

The Cocktail Garden

BY THE BONFIRE

Curry Leaf Paloma

60 ML (2 FL OZ) BLANCO TEQUILA

20 ML (¾ FL OZ) LEMON JUICE

30 ML (1 FL OZ) GRAPEFRUIT JUICE, PLUS A HALF-WHEEL TO GARNISH

20 ML (¾ FL OZ) GRAPEFRUIT SYRUP (PAGE 23)

5-6 CURRY LEAVES, PLUS 1 TO GARNISH

SODA WATER (CLUB SODA)

Shake all the ingredients, except the garnishes and soda water, with ice. Pass through a small fine-meshed strainer into a highball or tall glass containing fresh ice. Top with a dash of soda water and stir gently. Garnish with the half-wheel of grapefruit and the curry leaf.

Sage Advice

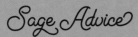

60 ML (2 FL OZ) WHITE RUM

30 ML (1 FL OZ) LIME JUICE

3 DASHES OF BITTERS (PREFERABLY ANGOSTURA)

20 ML (¾ FL OZ) SUGAR SYRUP (PAGE 18)

4 SAGE LEAVES

DRY SPARKLING WHITE WINE

Shake all the ingredients, except the wine, hard with ice. Pass through a small fine-meshed strainer into a martini or coupe glass and top with a splash of sparkling wine.

Kaffir Gimlet

60 ML (2 FL OZ) GIN

30 ML (1 FL OZ) LIME JUICE, PLUS A WHEEL TO GARNISH

30 ML (1 FL OZ) KAFFIR LIME SYRUP (PAGE 25)

Shake all the ingredients, except the lime wheel, with ice. Pass through a small fine-meshed strainer into a martini or coupe glass and add the lime wheel.

Tangerine Dream

45 ML (1½ FL OZ) TANGERINE OR MANDARIN JUICE, STRAINED
  (RESERVE THE SKIN)
100 ML (3½ FL OZ) SPARKLING WHITE WINE

Combine the tangerine or mandarin juice and sparkling wine in a mixing glass and gently stir so as not to break too many bubbles. Pour into a flute or wine glass. Hold the tangerine or mandarin skin over the glass and squeeze to release small bursts of citrus oil over the surface of the drink.

~

Among the citrus family — which has so many varieties and hybrids — tangerines can be difficult to find, depending on where you live. They are close to those varieties of mandarins that have brighter, reddish skin (the Murcott is one example). Use what you can get!

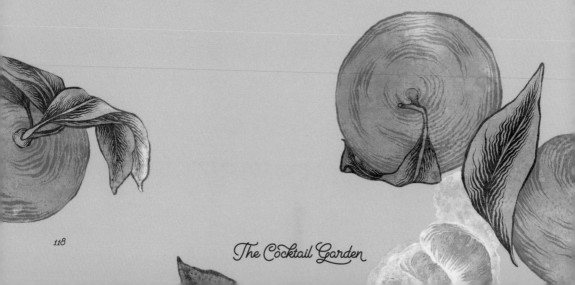

The Cocktail Garden

BY THE BONFIRE

Kale and Ginger Margarita

SEA SALT (OR SMOKED SEA SALT, FOR AN EARTHY WINTER TWIST)

WEDGE OF LIME, PLUS 30 ML (1 FL OZ) LIME JUICE

COIN OF GINGER, SLICED 1 CM (½ INCH) THICK

60 ML (2 FL OZ) BLANCO TEQUILA

30 ML (1 FL OZ) KALE JUICE

20 ML (¾ FL OZ) SUGAR SYRUP (PAGE 18)

Put a little salt in a shallow bowl. Wipe the lime wedge around the outside rim of a martini or coupe glass to wet it. Tilt the bowl slightly so the salt gathers up one end, and dip and turn the rim of the glass in the salt until it is coated all around. Shake off any excess. Muddle the ginger in the bottom of a shaker. Add the remaining ingredients and shake hard with ice. Pass through a small fine-meshed strainer into the glass.

The Cocktail Garden

Cumquat and Elderflower Collins

3–4 CUMQUATS

45 ML (1½ FL OZ) GIN

15 ML (½ FL OZ) ELDERFLOWER LIQUEUR SUCH AS ST GERMAIN
(OR ELDERFLOWER CORDIAL)

20 ML (¾ FL OZ) LEMON JUICE

60 ML (2 FL OZ) SODA WATER (CLUB SODA)

SPRIG OF MINT TO GARNISH

Gently muddle the cumquats in the bottom of a shaker, being careful not to pound too much (or you'll end up with an overly bitter drink without the subtle flavour of elderflower or the botanicals in the gin). Add ice and the remaining ingredients, except the soda water and mint, and shake. Pass through a small fine-meshed strainer into a collins or tall glass containing fresh ice and top with the soda water. Stir, and garnish with the mint.

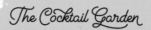

BY THE BONFIRE

Pomegranate and Thyme Highball

60 ML (2 FL OZ) BLENDED SCOTCH WHISKY

30 ML (1 FL OZ) POMEGRANATE JUICE

15 ML (½ FL OZ) POMEGRANATE MOLASSES

20 ML (¾ FL OZ) LEMON JUICE

SODA WATER (CLUB SODA)

SPRIG OF THYME TO GARNISH

Shake all the ingredients, except the soda water and thyme, with ice. Pass through a small fine-meshed strainer into a highball or tall glass containing fresh ice. Top with soda water and stir gently. Garnish with the thyme.

125

Winter G & T

30 ML (1 FL OZ) GIN

100 ML (3½ FL OZ) TONIC WATER

WEDGE OF PINK GRAPEFRUIT

2–3 LONG PEPPERS TO GARNISH (SEE NOTE BELOW)

Combine the gin and tonic in a large wine glass and add ice. Squeeze in the juice from the grapefruit wedge and drop the wedge into the glass, along with the peppers. Stir gently.

~

A juniper-heavy gin is what you want here (Tanqueray No. Ten, which also contains citrus, including grapefruit, would be ideal). Long pepper is a relation of common pepper consisting of many tiny pepper berries clustered on small brown spikes; it's slightly hotter than common pepper and has a numbing effect. If you can't find long pepper, use black, green, white or sichuan peppercorns instead.

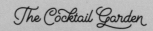

BY THE BONFIRE

Coffee Ritual

30 ml (1 fl oz) SPICED RUM

30 ml (1 fl oz) 666 AUTUMN BUTTER VODKA, OR BUTTER-WASHED VODKA (PAGE 32)

30 ml (1 fl oz) CHILLED ESPRESSO

20 ml (¾ fl oz) HONEY SYRUP (PAGE 18)

2 DROPS (OR ⅓ TEASPOON) CARDAMOM TINCTURE (PAGE 28)

2–3 COFFEE BEANS TO GARNISH

Shake all the ingredients, except the coffee beans, without ice to create a foam. Add ice and shake again. Pass through a small fine-meshed strainer into a martini or coupe glass and garnish with the coffee beans.

~

666 Autumn Butter Vodka from Tasmania is infused with local butter through a technique known as fat-washing. (Liquid fats such as oils or melted butter are mixed with spirits, and the mixture is left to infuse, adding richness and savoury flavour to the spirits. Then the mix is chilled, and the fat gets scooped off once solidified.) If you can't get your hands on this vodka, don't stress! There's a recipe on page 32 if you feel like throwing your hat in. Or use another quality vodka and your drink will still be super tasty.

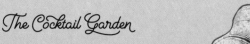

BY THE BONFIRE

Grapefruit Americano

30 ML (1 FL OZ) GRAPEFRUIT-INFUSED CAMPARI (PAGE 33)

30 ML (1 FL OZ) ROSSO VERMOUTH (PREFERABLY VERGANO AMERICANO)

90 ML (3 FL OZ) SODA WATER (CLUB SODA)

HALF-WHEEL OF GRAPEFRUIT TO GARNISH

Pour the Campari and vermouth into a tall glass over ice. Top with the soda water and stir gently. Add the wheel of grapefruit.

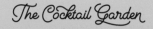

BY THE BONFIRE

For the
Garden Party

SPRING BRINGS PLENTY OF PROMISE AS WE TURN OUR BACKS ON WINTER AND LOOK TOWARDS THE SUMMER AHEAD. AND YET IT IS A LEAN SEASON IN FRUIT (WE CONTINUE MUNCHING ON APPLES AND PEARS DRAWN OUT OF COLD STORAGE, HUNGRILY WAITING FOR THE SOFT FRUIT TO BEGIN – THOUGH STRAWBERRIES HAVE A DELIGHTFUL HEAD START).

BUT LOOK TO THE GARDEN, AND TO SPRING'S ABUNDANCE OF VEGETABLES AND FLOWERS. JUST AS IN TEA, FLOWERS ARE EXCELLENT IN COCKTAILS, AS THEIR SUBTLE FLAVOUR IS NOT LOST WHEN COMBINED WITH SPIRITS. GENERALLY, THE BEST WAY OF GETTING THE FLAVOUR OF FLOWERS INTO A DRINK IS TO MAKE A SYRUP OUT OF THEM. SEE THE RECIPES FOR SYRUPS MADE WITH HIBISCUS, HONEYSUCKLE AND CHAMOMILE IN THE HOT-PROCESS SYRUP SECTION STARTING ON PAGE 18.

BUT DON'T LEAVE COCKTAILS JUST TO FRUITS, FLOWERS AND HERBS – THIS CHAPTER ALSO HAS RECIPES FEATURING SUGAR-SNAP PEAS, CUCUMBER AND SORREL.

Afternoon Apéro

90 ML (3 FL OZ) BLANC VERMOUTH (PREFERABLY REGAL ROGUE OR DOLIN)
WEDGE OF LIME
1 LEMON MYRTLE LEAF

Pour the vermouth into a wine glass over ice. Squeeze in the lime wedge and drop the wedge into the glass. Gently crack the lemon myrtle leaf to release the oils and stir through.

~

Lemon myrtle trees are native to Queensland, Australia, and are a fragrant and beautiful addition to gardens. If you can't find a source of fresh leaves, substitute with a short length of lemongrass, and gently press the lemongrass to release its oils.

FOR THE GARDEN PARTY

Mediterranean G & T

30 ML (1 FL OZ) GIN

10 ML (¼ FL OZ) SUZE (SEE PAGE 166)

100 ML (3½ FL OZ) TONIC WATER

WEDGE OF LEMON

HEALTHY SPRIGS OF ROSEMARY AND THYME TO GARNISH

Pour the gin and Suze into a large wine glass over ice. Top with the tonic water. Squeeze in the lemon wedge, drop the wedge into the glass and stir through. Garnish with the rosemary and thyme.

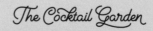

The Cocktail Garden

Banana Colada

60 ML (2 FL OZ) BANANA RUM (PAGE 33)

30 ML (1 FL OZ) PINEAPPLE JUICE

15 ML (½ FL OZ) LIME JUICE

30 ML (1 FL OZ) COCONUT CREAM

30 ML (1 FL OZ) COCONUT MILK

1 CUP ICE

Combine all the ingredients in a blender and blitz until smooth. Pour into a hurricane glass
(or alternatively a tall glass or wine glass).

~

*A kitsch drink deserves an equally kitsch garnish, so garnish with a miniature banana if
you're lucky enough to find some. Otherwise, use a slice of pineapple, a cocktail umbrella,
or even a smoking cinnamon stick (light one end, then blow out the flame but allow the stick
to keep smoking).*

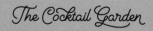

Southside Garden

1 LEBANESE (SHORT) CUCUMBER

60 ML (2 FL OZ) GIN

30 ML (1 FL OZ) LIME JUICE

20 ML (¾ FL OZ) SUGAR SNAP–PEA SYRUP (PAGE 21)

5 MINT LEAVES

EXTRA SPRIG OF MINT OR A BRIGHTLY COLOURED EDIBLE FLOWER
   TO GARNISH

Using a mandoline — or some mad knife skills — slice 2 paper-thin lengthways slices from the cucumber and wrap them around the inside of a rocks or short glass. Cut 3 thick slices from the remaining cucumber and muddle these in the bottom of a shaker. Add the remaining ingredients and shake with ice. Fill the cucumber-lined glass with crushed ice, and pass the cocktail through a small fine-meshed strainer into the glass. Garnish with a mint sprig or flower.

~

A southside is a favourite cocktail that is a refreshing mix of gin, lime and mint. This one has a spring garden twist, and instead of being served in a martini or coupe glass, it is served in a rocks or short glass over crushed ice so the drink lengthens as the ice melts.

The COCKTAIL *Garden*

FOR THE GARDEN PARTY

Strawberry and Tarragon Pisco Sour

60 ML (2 FL OZ) PISCO

30 ML (1 FL OZ) LEMON JUICE

30 ML (1 FL OZ) STRAWBERRY AND TARRAGON SYRUP (PAGE 24)

1–2 TEASPOONS EGG WHITE

Combine all the ingredients in a shaker and shake without ice to create a foam. Add ice and shake again. Pass through a small fine-meshed strainer into a martini or coupe glass.

FOR THE GARDEN PARTY

143

Rhubarb Cooler

45 ML (1½ FL OZ) WHITE RUM

15 ML (½ FL OZ) APEROL

15 ML (½ FL OZ) LEMON JUICE

15 ML (½ FL OZ) LIME JUICE

30 ML (1 FL OZ) RHUBARB SYRUP (PAGE 21)

6 MINT LEAVES, PLUS A SPRIG TO GARNISH

60 ML (2 FL OZ) SODA WATER (CLUB SODA)

LONG SLICE OF RHUBARB TO GARNISH

Shake all the ingredients, except the garnishes and soda water, with ice. Pass through a small fine-meshed strainer into a highball or tall glass containing fresh ice. Top with the soda water and stir gently. Garnish with the rhubarb and the sprig of mint.

FOR THE GARDEN PARTY

Full Bloom

3 SMALL CHUNKS OF PINEAPPLE

3 SMALL CHUNKS OF PAPAYA

1 TABLESPOON PASSIONFRUIT PULP,
  PLUS A WEDGE OF PASSIONFRUIT TO GARNISH

60 ML (2 FL OZ) CACHAÇA

15 ML (½ FL OZ) LIME JUICE

15 ML (½ FL OZ) LEMON JUICE

30 ML (1 FL OZ) HIBISCUS SYRUP (PAGE 19)

3 DASHES OF BITTERS (PREFERABLY PEYCHAUD'S)

DAISY TO GARNISH

Muddle the pineapple and papaya in the bottom of a shaker. Add the remaining ingredients, except the garnishes, and shake with ice. Pass through a small fine-meshed strainer into a rocks or short glass containing fresh crushed ice. Garnish with the passionfruit wedge and the daisy.

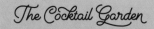

Honeydew Fix

4 CHUNKS OF HONEYDEW MELON

30 ML (1 FL OZ) LILLET BLANC

30 ML (1 FL OZ) VODKA

30 ML (1 FL OZ) LIME JUICE, PLUS A WHEEL TO GARNISH

10 ML (¼ FL OZ) SUGAR SYRUP (PAGE 18)

Muddle the honeydew in the bottom of a shaker. Add the remaining ingredients and shake with ice. Pass through a small fine-meshed strainer into a martini or coupe glass and add the lime wheel.

FOR THE GARDEN PARTY

Rhubarb Spritz

15 ML (½ FL OZ) RONDÒ APERITIVO

30 ML (1 FL OZ) RHUBARB SYRUP (PAGE 21)

90 ML (3 FL OZ) DRY LAMBRUSCO

30 ML (1 FL OZ) SODA WATER (CLUB SODA)

STRIP OF LEMON ZEST

Combine all the ingredients, except the lemon zest, in a wine glass and add ice. Stir gently. Squeeze the strip of zest to release its oils and add to the glass.

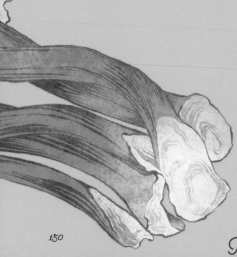

The Cocktail Garden

FOR THE GARDEN PARTY

Sorrel Smash

HANDFUL OF SORREL (SEE NOTE BELOW), PLUS A FEW EXTRA LEAVES
    TO GARNISH

15 ML (½ FL OZ) SUGAR SYRUP (PAGE 18)

60 ML (2 FL OZ) GIN

20 ML (¾ FL OZ) LEMON JUICE

20 ML (¾ FL OZ) GRAPEFRUIT JUICE, PLUS A HALF-WHEEL TO GARNISH

Muddle the sorrel with the sugar syrup in the bottom of a shaker. Add the gin and citrus juices and shake with ice. Pass through a small fine-meshed strainer into a short glass containing fresh ice. Garnish with the half-wheel of grapefruit and the extra sorrel leaves.

~

Sorrel looks like spinach but has a lemony flavour. One variety to look out for is the beautiful red-veined sorrel. Both common and red-veined sorrel will work in this recipe, as will the unrelated plant called wood sorrel or oxalis, which has a clover-like leaf and is a common weed.

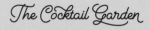

FOR THE GARDEN PARTY

Pine Gold

45 ML (1½ FL OZ) BOURBON

15 ML (½ FL OZ) APEROL

30 ML (1 FL OZ) LEMON JUICE

30 ML (1 FL OZ) PINEAPPLE AND TANGELO SYRUP (PAGE 22)

1-2 TEASPOONS EGG WHITE

2 DASHES OF BITTERS (PREFERABLY ANGOSTURA)

SLICE OF PINEAPPLE

HALF-WHEEL OF TANGELO

NASTURTIUM FLOWER

Shake all the ingredients, except the fruit slices and flower, without ice to create a foam. Shake again with ice. Pass through a small fine-meshed strainer into a short glass containing fresh ice and add the fruit slices and nasturtium.

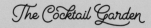

Honeysuckle 75

45 ML (1½ FL OZ) GIN

20 ML (¾ FL OZ) LEMON JUICE, PLUS A LONG, THIN STRIP OF LEMON ZEST

15 ML (½ FL OZ) HONEYSUCKLE SYRUP (PAGE 20)

60 ML (2 FL OZ) SPARKLING WHITE WINE

Shake the gin, lemon juice and honeysuckle syrup with ice. Strain (removing the ice) into a flute and top with the sparkling wine. Squeeze the strip of lemon zest to release its oils and add it to the glass.

~

Here is a honeysuckle twist on the French 75, a classic cocktail made with gin, Champagne, lemon juice and sugar. Honeysuckles are shrubs or vines with scented trumpet-shaped flowers that come in a range of colours, such as creamy white, yellow and peach. They are trellised along fences all around Sydney, Australia. Look out for honeysuckle in friends' gardens!

The Cocktail Garden

FOR THE GARDEN PARTY

Silkworm Sour

5 MULBERRIES, PLUS EXTRA TO GARNISH

45 ML (1½ FL OZ) RYE WHISKY

15 ML (½ FL OZ) AVERNA

30 ML (1 FL OZ) LEMON JUICE, PLUS A WEDGE TO GARNISH

20 ML (¾ FL OZ) SUGAR SYRUP (PAGE 18)

1–2 TEASPOONS EGG WHITE

Muddle the mulberries in the bottom of a shaker. Add the remaining ingredients, except the garnishes, and shake without ice to create a foam. Shake again with ice. Pass through a small fine-meshed strainer into a rocks or short glass containing fresh ice. Add a couple of extra mulberries and the wedge of lemon.

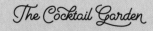

Chamomile Old Fashioned

60 ML (2 FL OZ) BLENDED SCOTCH WHISKY

15 ML (½ FL OZ) CHAMOMILE SYRUP (PAGE 20)

2–3 DROPS OF BITTERS (PREFERABLY DR ADAM ELMEGIRAB'S
   DANDELION AND BURDOCK BITTERS)

STRIP OF LEMON ZEST OR EDIBLE FLOWER TO GARNISH

Combine all the ingredients except the garnish in a mixing glass with ice and stir to chill the mixture. Strain (removing the ice) into a rocks or short glass. Add a fresh large cube of ice and garnish with the lemon or flower.

The Cocktail Garden

FOR THE GARDEN PARTY

The Bar Cart

MIXERS AND OTHER KEY INGREDIENTS

BITTERS Essentially liquors in themselves, bitters can be made up of dozens of different spices, herbs, fruits and other plant parts, infused or macerated in neutral high-proof spirits. They are often described as the 'salt and pepper' of the cocktail world — a seasoning used a few drops at a time to add an extra layer of depth. There are countless producers and styles, and each one is unique. Angostura is a common brand — it is made in Trinidad and has a distinctive taste (the recipe is a closely guarded secret, but its flavour hints towards herbs and spicy cinnamon). Peychaud's is another brand used in this book; it's more fruity and floral with notes of pepper and anise. You should feel free to try out other bitters that take your fancy.

EGG WHITE Bartenders have long known that the secret to a rich, creamy and smooth cocktail with a foam cap on top is egg white. The classic cocktail shaken with egg white is the whisky sour (whisky, lemon juice, sugar syrup, egg white). Generally all you need is a quarter of an egg white (1–2 teaspoons) per drink.

ICE Unless you like your drinks at room temperature, you're going to need plenty of ice when making cocktails. In fact, ice isn't just for chilling a drink — it's also one of the most important ingredients. The water from melted ice — from shaking or stirring — can make up 15–25 per cent of your final drink. Ice also plays another role in cocktails that are shaken, as it bruises soft ingredients such as herbs during the shaking, helping to release their flavour. You should be careful not to dilute drinks with melted ice too much. As a rule of thumb, the bigger the ice cubes, the better they are for shaking and stirring, as they melt more slowly. (Thin, cracked ice will melt too quickly without chilling the drink.) Many cocktails are made by shaking or stirring the ingredients with ice, then straining off that ice and pouring the drink over fresh ice cubes. This limits the dilution of the drink. Occasionally recipes call for crushed ice — one method for crushing ice is to fold ice cubes inside a clean tea towel (dish towel) and give them a few firm whacks with a rolling pin.

SODA WATER (CLUB SODA) Soda water is used to lengthen a drink and add a little sparkle. It's plain and refreshing, and doesn't get in the way of other seasonal flavours being showcased.

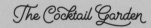

TONIC WATER The distinctive bitter ingredient of tonic water is quinine, derived from the bark of the South American cinchona tree (and other related trees). Quinine was used as a prophylactic against malaria and other tropical diseases in British India in the 19th century. The medicine was so bitter that officers discovered it tasted better mixed with soda water (club soda) and sugar — voila, tonic water was born. Not long after came the gin and tonic — officers began adding gin to their tonic, which improved the flavour again! These days tonic water has a light quinine bitterness as well as a refreshing citrus backbone. Each brand is unique, and you should use the one that you like and which works with your favourite gin — ideally one that is not overly sweet. Look out for Fentimans, which is drier than most tonic waters, and also Fever-Tree.

SPIRITS, LIQUEURS AND OTHER ALCOHOLS

To get technical, wines and beers are produced via fermentation. Spirits are produced via fermentation then distillation, which is the process of separating alcohol from water by carefully heating the fermented mixture (alcohol boils and vaporises at a lower temperature than water, making this possible). Spirits can be either plain (e.g. vodka), or flavoured (e.g. gin infused with juniper). Liqueurs are based on spirits but are sweetened, and are also richly flavoured with herbs, spices, fruits, flowers or even cream.

ABSINTHE Green spirit high in alcohol. Absinthe is flavoured with the leaves and flowers of wormwood — *Artemisia absinthium* — plus anise, fennel and other botanicals. Originating in Switzerland in the late 18th century, absinthe spread across Europe and the United States, becoming wildly popular among creatives, artists and writers. By the early 20th century it had been banned in most countries, accused of causing hallucinogenic and harmful effects. However, the offending chemical compound, thujone, is only present in the spirit in trace amounts, and later studies showed that the effects were greatly overstated and that absinthe is likely no more harmful than any other spirit. Since the 1990s absinthe has enjoyed a major revival.

AKVAVIT Scandinavian spirit (also spelt 'aquavit') produced from grain or potatoes and flavoured with caraway and other botanicals.

APEROL Bright orange *amaro* liqueur that includes sweet and bitter oranges and rhubarb in its ingredients (see **AVERNA** for more about the *amaro* family of liqueurs). Created in 1919 in the Veneto region of Italy, Aperol is the essential ingredient in the Venetian spritz, more commonly known around the world as the Aperol spritz (a simple combination of Aperol, Prosecco and soda water (club soda) on ice with a slice of orange). Aperol is light and low in alcohol, and less bitter than Campari (another Italian bitter liqueur).

AVERNA From the family of liqueurs called *amaro* (Italian for 'bitter'), which are typically consumed after a meal. *Amari* (plural) are made of neutral spirits or wine infused with herbs, roots, citrus and spices. Averna has been made in Sicily since the 19th century and has a dark colour and syrupy consistency.

BOURBON See **WHISKY**

BRÀULIO *Amaro* liqueur (see **AVERNA** for more about the *amaro* family of liqueurs) invented in 1875 in the town of Bormio, high up in the northern Italian alps. Infused with alpine herbs and roots, it has a distinctive and refreshing pine and menthol flavour.

CACHAÇA Brazilian spirit distilled from sugar cane juice, often compared to white rum. The most common variety of cachaça is white (unaged), but the premium variety is gold (aged in wooden barrels).

CAMPARI Italian liqueur invented in 1860 in the Piedmont region of Italy. It is an infusion of herbs and fruit characterised by its bitter orange flavour — similar to chinotto soft drink — and by its bright red colour. Commonly enjoyed in a spritz similar to the Aperol spritz (see **APEROL**), Campari is also an essential ingredient in the classic negroni cocktail.

CHARTREUSE Liqueur made by French monks in the Chartreuse mountains near Grenoble since the early 18th century — and still produced by monks. There are two main types of Chartreuse: the original green version, and a yellow version that is milder, a touch sweeter and lower in alcohol. Each is an infusion of 130 different plants and flowers.

ELDERFLOWER LIQUEUR A few elderflower liqueurs exist on the market, but St Germain is the most well known. It tastes of honey and flowers.

GIN Spirit generally made from grain and flavoured with juniper and other botanicals. Like many spirits (and liqueurs), gin began life as a medicine — called genever, it dates back to Belgium and the Netherlands in the 16th century. England started making its own version of the spirit the following century, and soon it exploded with popularity. Today some gins have dialled down the dominant juniper component and replaced it with more contemporary flavours, for example Hendrick's, which is infused with cucumber and roses. See also **SLOE GIN**.

JAPANESE PLUM WINE (*UMESHU*) *Ume* is a Japanese stone fruit, commonly referred to as a plum but actually closer to a sour apricot. The fruit is picked green and salted whole to make pickled plums called *umeboshi*, or steeped in Japanese alcohols such as sake or *shochu* to make *umeshu*. The best *umeshu* should be a balance of sweet and sour, and it is commonly enjoyed on ice or with soda water (club soda).

LAIRD'S APPLEJACK Apple-based spirit produced in the United States since 1780. Applejack was traditionally made by a primitive form of distillation called freeze distillation. Apple cider was left outside in winter, and the ice that formed on top was removed, leaving concentrated, unfrozen alcohol below (there are now health concerns around this process). These days, commercial applejack such as Laird's is produced by blending neutral spirits with apple brandy. Other apple-based spirits or brandies such as French calvados can be used instead.

LAMBRUSCO Sparkling red wine hailing from Emilia-Romagna (and the neighbouring region of Lombardy) in Italy. There are a number of styles produced, including a sweet Lambrusco that became very popular in the 1970s and 1980s; however for the recipes in this book, and for cocktails and spritzes in general, look for secco — dry Lambrusco.

LILLET BLANC From France's Bordeaux region, Lillet is an 'aromatised wine' with citrusy notes, made up of a blend of wine and liqueur. As well as the blanc (white) version, there is rosé and rouge. In France, Lillet is enjoyed as a classic aperitif, mostly served on the rocks or in a spritz.

MEZCAL Mexican agave spirit. Whereas tequila can only be made from blue agave, mezcal is made from upwards of thirty agave varieties. It is produced in eight regions of Mexico, although it's Oaxacan at heart. Production methods differ from tequila's — the agave is roasted in underground pits, which gives mezcal its distinctive smokiness.

PISCO Grape brandy produced in Chile and Peru, and famously used in the pisco sour, a cocktail made with lemon or lime, sugar and egg white.

PROSECCO Italian sparkling white wine produced in an area centring on the Veneto region of north-east Italy. The main variety of grape used is glera. Different to Champagne, Prosecco is made by a faster, cheaper method of secondary fermentation — this stage occurs in large tanks rather than in the bottle itself. This makes Prosecco a more affordable wine, and one designed to be drunk fresh and young.

RONDÒ APERITIVO Organic bitter liqueur from northern Italy. It sits between Campari and Aperol in bitterness and alcohol volume (Campari being the more bitter and higher in alcohol) and it makes for another great version of a spritz. If you can't find it, use Aperol or Campari instead.

RUM Spirit usually distilled from molasses, but sometimes also from fresh sugar cane juice. Rum comes in many varieties. **WHITE** (also known as blanco or silver) is aged just a short while and is mild and colourless, perfect for mixing in cocktails. **DARK** is at the other end of the scale, usually aged at length in wooden barrels and with rich colour and flavour, while **GOLD** lies somewhere in between. Both gold and dark rums are sometimes labelled as **AÑEJO** — the word means 'aged' in Spanish. **SPICED RUM** is another gold to dark-coloured rum flavoured with many different sweet spices, such as vanilla, cinnamon and cloves.

SCOTCH See **WHISKY**

SHERRY Fortified wine from the Andalusia region of southern Spain, which can be aged in two ways — either in the presence of oxygen, or under a layer of yeast called flor. Several varieties of grapes are used (although palomino grapes account for most sherries), and there are many styles. **FINO** is the driest and palest sherry, aged in barrels with flor. **AMONTILLADO** is first aged under flor, then oxidatively. It is lightly nutty in flavour and a superb cocktail match with rum and stone fruits! **OLOROSO** is aged oxidatively and for a longer period than amontillado. It is darker in colour and generally more punchy in flavour. **PEDRO XIMÉNEZ**, or PX, is a sweet dessert sherry made from grapes of the same name.

SLOE GIN Deep red liqueur from England made from gin and a small, dark variety of plum called a sloe or blackthorn berry.

SUZE French liqueur created in 1889 on the outskirts of Paris. Suze is made from an alpine plant called gentian, which has yellow flowers and large roots. The bitter roots are used as the flavouring; they have a lengthy history as a herbal medicine and are also the principal ingredient in a bunch of beverages including Aperol. In the glass, Suze strikes a balance between earthy, bitter, floral and fresh and has a distinctive lemon undertone. It is also low in alcohol at 15 per cent.

TEQUILA Mexican spirit distilled from the blue agave plant in a production area centring on the state of Jalisco (where you can find the town of Tequila). There are four main types of tequila. **BLANCO**, white or silver tequila is unaged, clear spirit; tequila in its rawest form. **REPOSADO** literally means 'rested'. This tequila is aged in wooden barrels between two months and a year, taking on a light golden hue. **AÑEJO** is aged from one to three years, while **EXTRA AÑEJO** is aged three years or more, becoming darker in colour the older it gets.

VERMOUTH Part of the 'aromatised wine' family, which are wines that are fortified with the addition of spirit and also infused with botanicals. The key botanical in vermouth is wormwood (it also features in absinthe). Broadly speaking, there are three styles of vermouth: **DRY**, plus two styles of sweet vermouth, either **BIANCO/BLANC** (white) or **ROSSO/ROUGE** (red). Side note: there are actually few red vermouths made with red wine and most get their colour from caramel. Check out Regal Rogue or Vergano Americano for vermouths made with red wine.

VODKA Vodka is a neutral spirit that is usually distilled from grains (corn, rye, barley) or potatoes. However, today there are examples made from grapes, quinoa and even sheep whey! The origin of vodka is a contentious issue between Russia and Poland, but the first written use of the word 'vodka' was in Poland in 1405. The aim of most vodkas is to be void of colour, aroma and taste (other than of the alcohol itself). For this reason vodka works extremely well in cocktails.

WHISKY Grain spirit produced from barley, corn, rye or wheat, and aged in wooden barrels. There are many different styles of whisky produced all over the world (in some places it is spelt 'whiskey'). **BOURBON** is an American whisky that must contain at least 51 per cent corn, and is mostly produced in Kentucky. The spirit ages in charred barrels, which gives colour and flavour. Its flavour is characterised by rich vanilla notes. **RYE WHISKY** is another chiefly American (and Canadian) product, with a flavour generally spicier and fruitier compared with bourbon. **SCOTCH WHISKY** hails from Scotland and is aged for a minimum of three years. It must contain at least a portion of malted barley (malting being the process of germinating grain briefly, then drying it, which creates enzymes that convert starches to sugars, assisting fermentation). Single malt scotch is the product of malted barley alone, as well as of a single distillery. Blended scotch is more common and is a mixture of whiskies made from malted barley and unmalted grain.

Index

The Cocktail Garden

The Cocktail Garden

About Adriana

Adriana is an illustrator born in Gosford, Australia. She has lived in the Blue Mountains, Newcastle, Sydney and other places where flowers and artists seem to thrive. At the heart of Adriana's work is a lifelong passion for botanical illustration.

As an illustrator, artist and designer, her work encompasses the diverse fields of publishing, fine arts, film and advertising.

This is Adriana's third book with Hardie Grant. She has previously illustrated two successful colouring books, *Where the Wildflowers Grow* and *The Garden of Earthly Delights*.

About Ed

Taking it upon himself at age sixteen to develop a cocktail list for one hundred guests at his cousin's engagement party, Ed has gone on to become a bartender and restaurateur in a career spanning over a decade. He started behind the bar at late-night joint Cargo Bar, and later opened up The Passage Bar with Andy Emerson. Ed's passion for drinks has seen him develop award-winning wine and cocktail lists for ACME and Bar Brosé (the latter was awarded Best Wine List in the 2016 Australian Liquor Industry Awards).

Ed's fresh, flavour-driven recipes haven't been simplified for this book; this is how he makes drinks at work and at home. He believes that using produce at the height of its season is the best way to maximise flavour, and that using locally grown produce supports local agriculture — super important amid ever-growing globalisation.

'As a bartender your job is just to be creative, and to find a balance between ingredients,' says Ed. 'I generally despise [artificial] liqueurs. My philosophy has always been, why use a raspberry liqueur when you can make your own raspberry syrup?'

Bar Brosé is Ed's current home — a late-night dining venue known for its French-inspired menu, natural wines, and cocktails made with seasonal produce.

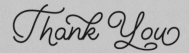

Thank You

FROM ADRIANA

Firstly, a massive thank you to the team at Hardie Grant for all their hard work, and particularly to Fran Berry for the inception of the idea.

Thank you to my dear friend Silvana Azzi Heras for her years of unwavering support, advice and mentorship, and for lending her very talented eye to finesse the design of this book.

To my family for their constant belief in my abilities, particularly my parents, Bryan and Sally Picker, my aunt and uncle Margo and Geoff Coltheart and, most importantly, my incredible brother, Andrew Picker, who is my strongest advocate.

To Pat Nourse for his friendship, early adoption of my illustrations and for his wonderful foreword.

To Anna Westcott, Alice Kimberley, Andrew Steele, Matthew Sweiboda, Pauline Georges, James Jirat Patradoon, Rebecca Castle, Nikki To, Emma Hetherington and, particularly on this occasion, Roy Leibowitz and Josie Grant — for helping me stay sane, as an extroverted person, having chosen a pretty solitary career. You are all my heart.

Finally, thank you to Ed. Working with you has been a pure joy.

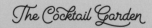

FROM ED

First and foremost, Adriana. Thank you for inviting me along on this ride! I have been in total awe of your illustrations for some time, and I'm incredibly privileged and grateful to be able to work on a project with you.

My sincerest gratitude to Loran McDougall, Rachel Pitts and the rest of the team at Hardie Grant for your guidance and support.

To my business partners at ACME and Bar Brosé (Andy, Cam, Mitch and Analiese), thank you for your patience and understanding through the writing process.

Special shout out to Victoria Pearson for generously giving your time and some rather eloquent suggestions.

And last but not least, my parents, Jane and Colin, and brother, Ollie. I am so fortunate to have your unwavering support and love.

Published in 2017 by Hardie Grant Books, an imprint of
Hardie Grant Publishing

Hardie Grant Books (Melbourne)
Building 1, 658 Church Street
Richmond, Victoria 3121

Hardie Grant Books (London)
5th & 6th Floors
52–54 Southwark Street
London SE1 1UN

hardiegrantbooks.com

A Cataloguing-in-Publication entry is available from the
catalogue of the National Library of Australia at www.nla.gov.au

The Cocktail Garden
ISBN 978 1 74379 285 8

Publishing Directors: Fran Berry and Jane Willson
Managing Editor: Marg Bowman
Project Editor: Loran McDougall
Editor: Rachel Pitts
Design Manager: Mark Campbell
Production Manager: Todd Rechner
Production Coordinator: Rebecca Bryson

Colour reproduction by Splitting Image Colour Studio
Printed in China by 1010 Printing International Limited